A Question of Science Book

CAN YOU HITCH A RIDE ON A COMET?

by Sidney Rosen
illustrated by Dean Lindberg

Carolrhoda Books, Inc./Minneapolis

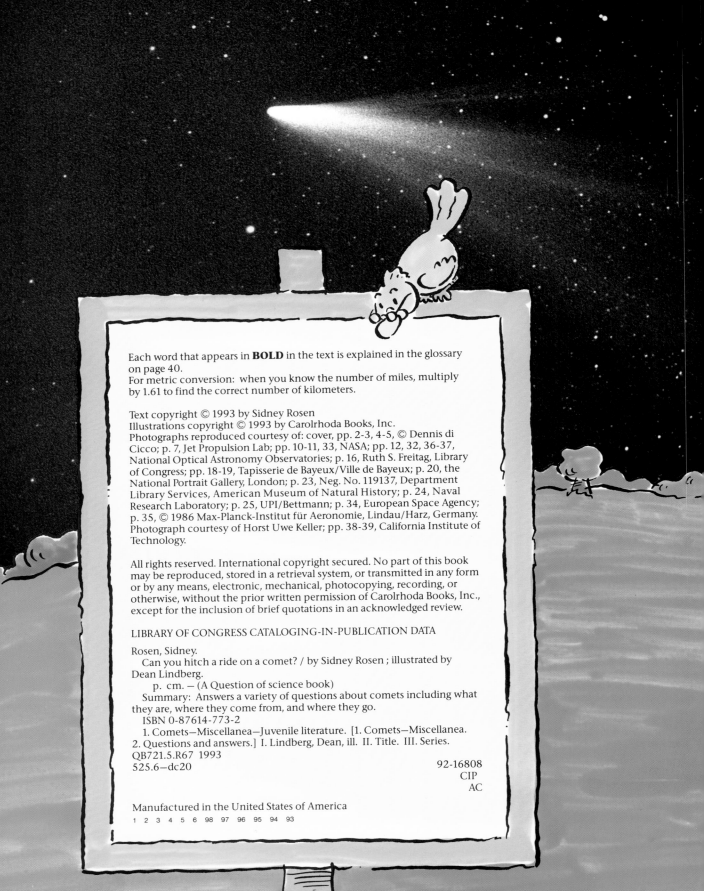

Each word that appears in **BOLD** in the text is explained in the glossary on page 40.
For metric conversion: when you know the number of miles, multiply by 1.61 to find the correct number of kilometers.

Text copyright © 1993 by Sidney Rosen
Illustrations copyright © 1993 by Carolrhoda Books, Inc.
Photographs reproduced courtesy of: cover, pp. 2-3, 4-5, © Dennis di Cicco; p. 7, Jet Propulsion Lab; pp. 10-11, 33, NASA; pp. 12, 32, 36-37, National Optical Astronomy Observatories; p. 16, Ruth S. Freitag, Library of Congress; pp. 18-19, Tapisserie de Bayeux/Ville de Bayeux; p. 20, the National Portrait Gallery, London; p. 23, Neg. No. 119137, Department Library Services, American Museum of Natural History; p. 24, Naval Research Laboratory; p. 25, UPI/Bettmann; p. 34, European Space Agency; p. 35, © 1986 Max-Planck-Institut für Aeronomie, Lindau/Harz, Germany. Photograph courtesy of Horst Uwe Keller; pp. 38-39, California Institute of Technology.

LIBRARY OF CONGRESS CATALOGING-IN-PUBLICATION DATA

Rosen, Sidney.
 Can you hitch a ride on a comet? / by Sidney Rosen ; illustrated by Dean Lindberg.
  p. cm. — (A Question of science book)
 Summary: Answers a variety of questions about comets including what they are, where they come from, and where they go.
  ISBN 0-87614-773-2
  1. Comets—Miscellanea—Juvenile literature. [1. Comets—Miscellanea. 2. Questions and answers.] I. Lindberg, Dean, ill. II. Title. III. Series.
QB721.5.R67 1993
525.6—dc20   92-16808
                                                                  CIP
                                                                  AC

Manufactured in the United States of America
1 2 3 4 5 6 98 97 96 95 94 93

What is a comet?

A comet is a visitor from outer space that enters the **Solar System.**

A visitor? You mean like someone from another planet?

No, a comet isn't a person. As far as we can tell, a comet is just a big ball of dirty snow and ice that has come from the very, very cold parts of outer space.

Could I really hitch a ride on a comet?

Well, you would have to leave the Earth and travel out in space. And even if you could catch up with a comet, you might not like the ride.

What kind of ride would it be?

BRRRR!

Not a very comfortable one, I'm afraid. First, you would be freezing cold. Then, when the comet got near the Sun, you would be boiling hot.

Where did we get the word comet?

From the Greek word *kome*, which means *hair*. That's because the streamers of a comet's tail looked like strands of hair to ancient Greeks. Other people agree. In the African country of Zaire, the Tshi people call comets "hair stars."

WHEW!

Why such a big change?

Because comets come from way out in space, far away from the Sun's heat. Comets make a trip around the Sun, warm up, and then go back out.

Do comets ever come back again?

Yes. But it takes most comets hundreds, or even thousands, of years to return.

How will I know a comet when I see one?

Until it gets close to the Sun, a comet looks just like
a little dot of light. You need a **telescope** to see it.

So is it like a star?

It may look like a star, but a comet doesn't give off
its own light as a star does. The light you see is the
Sun's light bouncing off the comet. Sunlight hits the
ice in a comet and is reflected back, the same way
light is reflected by a mirror.

*But comets don't always look like points of light,
do they?*

No, when a comet gets close to the Sun, bits of the comet's surface begin melting and streaming away from the comet like a long tail.

TAIL
(SPACE DUST AND GAS)

the PARTS OF A COMET

That tail always points away from the Sun.

Why does it point away from the Sun?

Why don't comets melt when they get close to the Sun?

During that part of a comet's trip, some of the snow and ice does melt. Of course, as soon as a comet gets away from the Sun, the melted part refreezes. In making trip after trip, a comet will slowly wear down to nothing. But comets spend most of their time away from the Sun's warmth. All that time in space's deep freeze helps some comets survive for thousands of years.

HEAD (FROZEN ICE AND SPACE DUST)

The Sun's light and heat are so strong they push bits of the comet's surface out into space.

How did people discover comets?

Sometimes comets pass close enough to the Earth for the comet and its tail to be visible to the naked eye. Ancient Chinese sky watchers saw comets 3,000 years ago. Comets were also seen and described by early Aztecs in Mexico and by the Incas in Peru.

Did it scare people when they saw a comet in the sky?

You bet! Until not too long ago, when people saw a comet, they always thought it meant that some terrible disaster was going to happen.

For instance, in the year 1066, King William of Normandy—that's part of France—crossed the English Channel and attacked the English army. A comet appeared in the night sky just before the battle.

How do we know people saw a comet all those years ago?

We have pictures to prove it. The story of the battle was woven soon afterwards into a great wall hanging called the Bayeux (bye-YUH) Tapestry. Part of it, as you can see, shows a great comet with several tails flying across the sky.

That's awesome! But who won the battle?

King Harold of England was killed and his army lost. The English people blamed their loss on the comet. Of course, the winner, King William, probably thought the comet had brought *him* good luck.

Did that comet ever come back?

Yes. This comet passes by the Earth on its round trip every 75 years. It's called Halley's (HAL-eez) Comet.

Why is this comet called Halley's?

"HALLEY rhymes with VALLEY!"

Because Edmond Halley, an Englishman, was the first to predict when the comet would appear.

He saw the comet in 1682. From what he knew
about how comets travel, he figured out the exact
number of years it would take for the comet to return.
And 75 years later, in 1757, the comet was seen again
near the Earth. Halley had died by that time, but in
his honor the comet was given his name.

How did Halley know when the comet would be
coming back?

His friend, the great English scientist Isaac Newton, had figured out how to predict the **orbits** of planets and comets.

What's an orbit?

How are comets different from shooting stars?

Shooting stars are **meteors,** small bits of dust and rock that travel through space. Sometimes meteors enter Earth's **atmosphere** and burn up. You see them as a sudden white streak across the night sky. Comets are much larger bodies that, like planets, move around the Sun. You only see a shooting star for a second or two. But comets may be visible night after night on their journey through space.

It's the path taken by one object in the sky around another object. Each year, the Earth takes one trip around the Sun. The Earth's path around the Sun is called its orbit. Some comets also orbit the Sun.

Do comets ever crash into the Sun?

Yes, there's always a chance that will happen. In 1979, one of our spaceships took pictures of a comet that hit the Sun and was burned up.

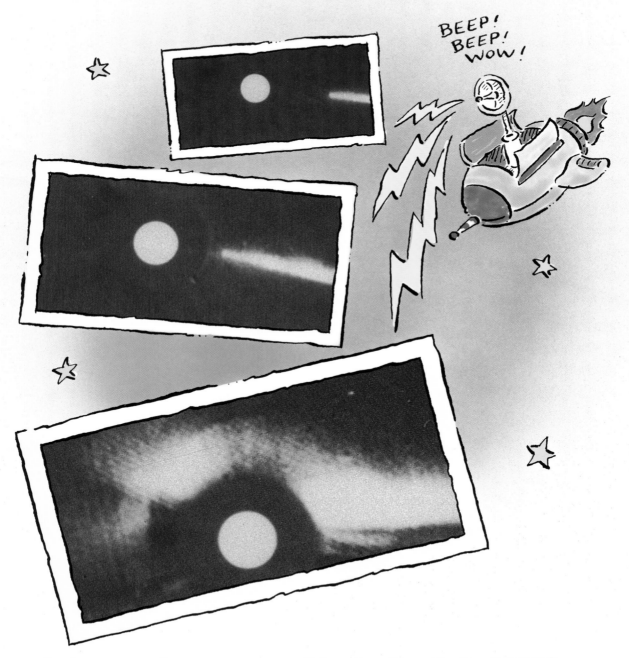

Is it true that a comet hit the Earth in 1908?

In that year, in a part of Siberia near the Tunguska River, there was a mysterious explosion. No one was killed, but trees were blown down for miles. The explosion might have been caused by a small piece of a comet that blew up just before hitting the Earth. Or it might have been a large meteor. No one knows for sure.

What are the chances that a comet will hit the Earth sometime soon?

The chances of that happening are very, very small—
maybe once in about a million years. The Earth is a
pretty small target. And compared to Earth, comets
are very, very tiny.

Imagine putting an apple on a fencepost and then
flinging small stones at the apple from a mile away.
What are your chances of hitting the apple even once?

Probably not too great. There is almost no chance that a person on Earth will ever be hit by a comet.

How are comets made?

We really don't know. It was once thought that they were shot out from volcanoes.

Do people still think that?

No, we now know that's nonsense. A volcano could never shoot rocks and dust all the way into space.

Now scientists like the idea suggested in 1950 by a Dutch **astronomer** named Jan Oort. He saw comets as millions of pieces of space rubbish all moving in a great ring at an enormous distance from the Sun. This ring is called the **Oort comet cloud.**

How do comets get out of this ring?

> How can a star "nudge" a comet?
>
> Scientists believe that a star's **gravity** can affect comets in the Oort comet cloud. Gravity is an attracting force between objects. The Earth's gravity keeps us stuck on the ground. Try jumping high up in the air. You'll always come back down because of the pull of gravity. Scientists picture the Oort comet cloud as being not too far from stars. Once every so often, a comet will be "nudged" out of the cloud by the pull of gravity from a nearby star.

Oort thought that, every once in a while, a nearby star might nudge a few objects out of the cloud to fly toward the Sun.

Can we see the Oort comet cloud?

No one has ever seen it. The nearest part may be 50 trillion (that's 50,000,000,000,000) miles away.

Maybe one of our rocket ships going out toward the stars will send back a picture of it someday. Until then, we can use the idea of the Oort comet cloud to explain where comets come from.

What happens to a comet once it gets out of the Oort comet cloud?

That depends on how close it goes to planets. Jupiter, the biggest planet, probably affects what comets do more than any other planet. Jupiter's gravity can slow a comet down or make it go faster. If the comet is slowed down, it will go around the Sun and return in a fairly short time, just as Halley's Comet does.

But sometimes Jupiter's gravity can act like a base-ball bat that gives the comet a home-run whack! The comet speeds up, whizzes around the Sun, and rushes way off into space—like Comet Kohoutek. The whack of gravity can even knock a comet right out of the Solar System. Then it would never return.

Did any of our spaceships ever get a good look at a comet?

Yes. In 1986, Halley's Comet
passed by Earth. Several
countries sent up spaceships
to meet the comet.

*Did they try
to hitch a ride
with Halley?*

No. But the spaceships did send back pictures. A European spaceship called *Giotto* got about 200 miles from the comet and sent back marvelous pictures. They show a cloud of shining dust around the comet's head.

Photos taken from Earth show Halley's Comet
streaking through the night sky.

*Wow! Well, if I can't hitch a ride on a comet,
will I at least be able to see Halley's Comet
when it comes around again?*

Children who will be your age in the year 2061 will
certainly see it. And you might, too.

So plan to hang around!

GLOSSARY

astronomer: A scientist who is interested in explaining how the universe works, and who observes and studies the planets, stars, and galaxies for this purpose

atmosphere: All the gases that surround the Earth and other planets and stars

gravity: The force that makes objects attract each other. The Earth's gravity is so strong it keeps us stuck to Earth.

meteors: Hot, glowing objects that flash through the Earth's atmosphere. Meteors are usually smaller than comets.

Oort comet cloud: A great "cloud" of comets that possibly exists far from the Earth and from which comets can move out into orbits around the Sun

orbit: The path of one object around another, such as a comet around the Sun

Solar System: The Sun and all the bodies that move around it—planets, moons, comets, asteroids, and meteors

telescope: An instrument used by astronomers to observe planets, stars, comets, and galaxies